How to Stop C and Take Action!

by

Patrick. Miller

Copyright © 2020 by Scottsdale Book Publishing

All rights reserved. No part of this publication may be reproduced, distributed, or transmitted in any form or by any means, including photocopying, recording, or other electronic or mechanical methods, without the prior written permission of the publisher, except in the case of brief quotations embodied in critical reviews and certain other noncommercial uses permitted by copyright law. For permission requests, write to the publisher, addressed, "Attention: Permissions Coordinator," at the address below.

Scottsdale Book Publishing
Scottsdale, Arizona

ISBN: 9798648018471

Published in the United States of America

Table of Contents

- INTRODUCTION: HOW TO GET MOTIVATED 7
- CHAPTER 1: REMOVE FAILURE FROM YOUR PSYCHOLOGY 8
- CHAPTER 2: MAKE A SINGLE GOAL 10
- CHAPTER 3: LOOKING FOR INSPIRATION 12
- CHAPTER 4: GET YOURSELF EXCITED 14
- CHAPTER 5: BUILDING ANTICIPATION 16
- CHAPTER 6: PUBLIC COMMITMENT 18
- CHAPTER 7: RUMINATE ON IT DAILY 20
- CHAPTER 8: POST YOUR GOAL 22
- CHAPTER 9: GAIN SUPPORT 24
- CHAPTER 10: UNDERSTAND THAT THERE ARE AN EBB AND FLOW 26
- CHAPTER 11: DO NOT GIVE UP 28
- CHAPTER 12: BEGIN A LITTLE 30
- CHAPTER 13: BUILD ON SMALL SUCCESSES 32
- CHAPTER 14: CALL FOR HELP 33
- CHAPTER 15: THINK ABOUT THE BENEFITS AND NOT THE DIFFICULTIES 35
- CHAPTER 16: REPLACE NEGATIVE THOUGHT WITH POSITIVE ONES 37
- CHAPTER 17: AIM HIGHER 38
- CHAPTER 18: KILL PROCRASTINATION 40
- CHAPTER 19: SETTING SPECIFIC GOALS 42
- CHAPTER 20: MAKE HABITS YOUR MOTIVATIONS 44

INTRODUCTION: HOW TO GET MOTIVATED

What do you want? What are your goals? What are you after? What outcome are you looking for? Are finding it difficult to complete the tasks you have set out to do, and this scares you? This, contrary to what you may think, is not a display of lack of intelligence or an inability to focus. It may be that you are probably suffering from a lack of motivation.

Without motivation, without the drive and the desire to do anything, you might just find yourself in a spot with life passing you by. Even the most motivated of us can feel pretty down and apathetic. The scary thing about these periods is that we might be so into the slump that we cannot even seem to think about making positive changes.

Losing motivation can be a slippery slope or a sharp decline. It may start off with something as innocuous as skipping exercise routines to essential things like receiving disappointing news. There are several ways to get back on the horse and find the

motivation to make the substantial changes you always dreamed about.

CHAPTER 1: REMOVE FAILURE FROM YOUR PSYCHOLOGY

Humans, being what we are, change, and adapt over the years. In the words of one of the best evolutionary scientists. Charles Darwin, he said, *"it is not the strongest of the species who survive, it is the one most adaptable to change."* From the cradle, we have learned through trial and error to walk, talk, and grow into the fully functioning adults we are today. In all that time, words have been said repeatedly to us from family, friends, teachers, neighbors, classmates, bullies, crushes, that have sunk into our psyche. The repeated words have cemented themselves in us, making us believe that is who we are.

People grew up around negative words, and negative mindsets now believe themselves to be failures. As their mistakes were always thrown in their faces, they were often unable to make a clear separation

between their errors and their identities. You hear them make statements like *"I'm so stupid"* instead of *"I just did something stupid."* Making constant demotivating comments like those sticks were you, and you begin to manifest what is not you. Taking into consideration the words of the Los Angeles- based psychologist Crystal I. Lee, *Failure is seen as an opportunity to learn and grow. Failure is a chance to be embraced, analyzed, and picked apart, rather than something to run away from."*

To gain motivation to improve on yourself and pursue excellence, you need to change your mentality and rid yourself of negative thoughts and feelings. Understand that just because you are failing at one thing does not make you a failure. Like Louai Rahal wrote based on the work of the psychologist Carol Dweck. *"when we believe that abilities are fixed (fixed mindset), we interpret failure as evidence for lack of ability, and we stop trying. When we believe that abilities can be*

stretched with learning (growth mindset), we perceive failures as opportunities for learning. We reflect on failures to stretch our abilities" Reiterating positive statements and thoughts to yourself will do wonders to your self-esteem and boost your self-worth. You will begin to see yourself in a new light, and you will find yourself motivated and excited.

CHAPTER 2: MAKE A SINGLE GOAL

As surprising as it may seem, one of the reasons for lack of motivation is trying too hard and trying to do too much too fast. When you have too many coals on fire, and you have stretched yourself too thin, you may find it challenging to even find the desire to do anything. You end up producing subpar works that leave you frustrated. We, as humans, are nothing but a society of multitaskers. We are often doing more than we can handle. When we multitask, we are much less efficient than we think as our minds are scattered, and thus our output is mediocre. We often rush through a task just to check one chore off the list, and so many times, we do not put our best foot forward. We are not enjoying the process, nor are we taking a moment to relish in the end product. We are usually too busy moving on to the next task.

With many things demanding our attention, to find motivation requires creating a laser-like focus on the goal we have set out to achieve. The trick to multitasking is that for you to perform two tasks at the same time, one of them must be automatic, thus requiring no focus or thought, and both tasks must require different brain processing. An example of this is reading and listening to music without paying attention to the lyrics.

In situations when either of those conditions cannot be met, what you should do is streamline your goals and objectives. There are certainly those you can put on a backburner as well as tasks that require a little more thought. Why not build your priorities and stick to your plan of starting with an objective a day or a goal at a time? You should clear all forms of distractions like your cellphones or even the people around you by staying in a quiet, secluded place. When you have completed your set goal, you can then move to the next one on the list. That way,

you conserve your time and energy, not burning the candle at both ends, and you find yourself always motivated.

CHAPTER 3: LOOKING FOR INSPIRATION

Inspiration is a mental and emotional state when your consciousness is heightened, and your awareness is open to higher vibrations. It is creativity expressing itself through your soul and mind. Sometimes inspiration strikes unexpectedly, and when it does, you feel alive, energized and filled with the desire to make changes and make things happen. There are other days when inspiration just seems to be lost. On those days, you feel lost, empty, lacking zest, creativity, energy, and even the will to do basic things.

When there is no inspiration to make things happen, there is no motivation. To remain motived, there are certain things that you can do to find the inspiration you need. You do not always have to dig deep to get inspired. First, clear your mind. It is essential to keep an open mind to welcome your next big idea. Look at the world with a child's eye,

with no judgment, with no resentment, with appreciation, attention, and mindfulness.
You can read books, magazines, articles, or blogs for inspiration on how to get motivated for your next project. You can also turn to these around you for inspiration. There are undoubtedly other activities you can do like yoga, meditation, a brisk walk, or jogging to get the juices flowing and relax your mind for the arrival of the next big idea.

Do not give up on yourself when the well seems to have run dry, it happens to everyone. Accept your current situation and take a break from yourself, this will allow your brain to refocus and reboot. Try to do something different, something spontaneous, either alone or with a group of friends.

When you have a task to do but cannot seem to motivate yourself to begin, you can just start working on it. Yes, working without inspiration is dull and boring and just tiring. Still, if you start, with time and effort, inspiration will suddenly appear.

CHAPTER 4: GET YOURSELF EXCITED

It is one thing to have a goal, it is quite different from being excited about it. When there is no zeal, it is challenging to complete said task efficiently. One of the best ways to be motivated is to get yourself excited about the work you want to do. It may seem necessary or even unhelpful information. Still, if you are passionate about your project, no matter how seemingly unimportant it looks like to you. It will get you revved up to have a fantastic day and remain motivated for the rest of it.

How do I get excited about something that I am not motivated about, you may ask? Well, why do not you start by talking about it? Pitching the idea is one of the best ways to get yourself excited about your project and get yourself motivated. You may get scared when you come up with the idea that seems bigger

than you, a project you may seem to have grown beyond who you are. The best way to get your motivation back is to imagine the end result.

Then talk about it with a friend, and together you can fix all the pain points of the project. Pitch your ideas again to relevant partners who can help you achieve your dreams. From there, you begin to build excitement, and you get motivated to do your task. All you should do is keep the ball rolling, and you will always find yourself motivated.

As you keep working on the project, your excitement may wane. Do not panic. That is entirely normal. Rather than let it scare you off, why not use that as a period to learn more, not just about yourself, but about your team members, if you have one. If you do not, you ask yourself, *"Have I learned everything there is to learn about this project I am undertaking?"* Once you begin learning again, your excitement and motivation will return.

CHAPTER 5: **BUILDING ANTICIPATION**

Building anticipation for yourself seems like a stupid idea, right? Well, I assure you it is not. Just like it happens wit's launching an event or a product when you build anticipation for something, you are continually motivated and eager to work on said project. By building anticipation, you are subconsciously gearing yourselves up for a positive outcome. This will encourage you to get started and achieve that successful ending you have been thinking about.

According to the phenomenon known as the 'Pygmalion Effect,' which was named after a Greek myth about a sculptor who fell in love with a statue he carved, grand expectations produce high productivity. The opposite of that is the 'Golem Effect, ' which is loosely translated to mean low expectations provides deficient performance. To avoid

negative 'self-fulfilling prophecies' and pessimistic talks, you need to get psyched about whatever it is you are working on. Teach yourself a lesson in productivity, and this will help boost your expectations for your project and will, in turn, yield positive outcomes.

Just because you have an idea now does not mean you should start working on it right away. Stir the pot for a little while, delay gratification. Set a date to begin working on your project on your calendar; it may be a week, two weeks, or even a month. Marking a set a time for the beginning of a project will help build anticipation. In the meantime, you can start building and writing out a plan to implement your new idea. Work on finessing your program and working out the kinks. By delaying the execution of your policy, you have successfully motivated yourself to execute the project. Building anticipation also has the added advantage of making sure you do not have too many coals in the fire.

CHAPTER 6: PUBLIC COMMITMENT

We all want to be known as a person who keeps his or her word. Psychologists refer to this as the 'rule of commitment' or the 'norm of commitment.' By publicly announcing your goal to friends and family, you are going the extra mile in ensuring that you stay committed and motivated to complete your task, whatever it may be, whether it is sticking to a new diet or exercising more or writing more or maybe you are just trying to stop smoking.

Committing to something is more than being interested in something. It means forgetting about every other thing and pouring all of your energy and attention on one clear objective on one defining goal. Commitment is a pledge to the dedication, the discipline, the patience, and the determination you need to succeed at the task ahead, not minding the discomfort and the difficulties, the problems

and the complications, the troubles, and the inconveniences you will undoubtedly experience along your journey. Commitment is all about never backing down from your word, no matter what.

It is believed that once we have made an open pledge about something, we feel obligated either by social pressure and/or internal psychological pressure to stick to it. Whenever the passion that drove you to begin this journey seems to be waning, the thought of not wanting to disappoint will fan the flames of your love until it burns bright again within you. Whenever motivation appears below, and you are tempted to give up, the fact that there are people -friends, families, coworkers, or even audience for those who made a public commitment in their blogs or social media handles- who will hold you accountable for your earlier words and remind you the motivation why you started it may be the push you need to complete your task. It will help you understand the fact that you have

to make this work and you cannot quit. You can also provide them with weekly updates on the progress you are making.

CHAPTER 7: **RUMINATE ON IT DAILY**

One of the best ways to get motivated is to think daily about your project. By stretching your mental muscles, you will not only increase your powers of intent and focus, your big dreams and goals will also take shape in your mind, growing bigger and bigger, modifying and correcting itself in places where needed. Ruminating on your ideas often allows you to improve them in a laser-like manner and streamline your goals. There is a correlation between thought and action. The more you think about something, the more energized you are at pulling it off, and so it is more likely going to come true.

To do that, you can set daily reminders and make notes when a thought comes. Committing as little of your time as five minutes to your project is enough to get you motivated to complete your task. This will

allow you the opportunity to know exactly what it takes to achieve your goals. When you always modify your goals to fit the current times, you will be at the top of your game and not get sidelined with changes or left behind in the ever-changing fast-paced world.

When you continuously ruminate on your goals, it helps you know where you are going and what your limits are. It enables you to adjust your goals and push you to expand your boundaries. For instance, if you wish to write the next bestselling book, by continually ruminating on your grand idea, you can embellish, add, remove, adjust until you have a finished product. You add the modern-day devices that are released every day and remove catchphrases that go out of style as quickly as they come. As you write and ruminate, you have a finished product that is every bit as great as you want it to be.

CHAPTER 8: **POST YOUR GOAL**

A picture, as you very well know, is said to be worth a thousand goals. As humans, during ceremonies that seem to mark the end of one thing and the beginning of another like during new year's or on our birthdays or even when tossing a coin into an old well, we make grand plans and dream big dreams. When inspiration strikes, we are very excited, and we believe we have the idea that will revolutionize the world as we know it or will at least change our lives for the better. Then life happens and the magic of the new year is gone and the high spirits of the birthday are gone, and so we forget about our ideas and big dreams. We simply lose inspiration and the motivation to do whatever it is we set out to do.

One of the ways to continually remain motivated and not let your dreams fall by the

wayside is to have a visual representation of what your goal is. You can also write out your goals in printed forms and post them around your house like on the refrigerator or your walls. You can also post them in your workplace if your goal is work-related.

Some people even make them into mantras or slogans like *"hot summer banging body"* or *"a word a day, a thousand pages it makes."* They then post it at home or at work, on their computer desks or their workout benches.

This will help motivate you to complete your task and keep the excitement going. For those who like visual aids, a picture of your goal also helps. You can make charts, tables, lists, of what you want to achieve, projected estimates of cost, time, man-hours, and so on. This will help to keep you motivated to complete your goal.

There are reports which suggest visualization of the success of your goal helps in boosting the spirit and increasing morale.

Take a moment to imagine the future. Create a mental image of the moment of your success with as much detail as possible. Engage all of your senses in creating this image. Who is with you? What are you feeling right now? What are you wearing? What smell is in the air? What do you hear? Creating your mental success image will do wonders for your drive and encourage you more than anything to continue working until you achieve success.

CHAPTER 9: **GAIN SUPPORT**

Like John Butman, the author of

Breaking out: How to Build Influence in a World of Competing Ideas, says, "it is hard to get people to listen to your idea, to understand your idea and to take action." However, no man is an island, and you need support to get your ideas off the ground. You need to build your support base, people who will encourage you and help you in pushing your agenda forward. In an office or workplace setting, John Butman recommends the 'cocktail party test" to gain the support of your coworkers.

It is a setting where you find colleagues who might be interested in your idea. They may be close coworkers, or they may even be in a completely different department, and you broach your concept to them informally and casually present your

idea to them. Listen to their feedback, their questions, observations, and opposing views. Like Susan Ashford, professor of management and organization at Michigan's Ross School of Business, says, "be sure to integrate their feedback into your game plan. It is a process of iteration and figuring out what works." By doing so, you also gain their support and make them invested in your plan. You have earned for yourself people who will support you and encourage you every step of the way.

For those grand ideas that require the support of your bosses or investors, you need to strategize how to meet with them and how to sell your product to the higher-ups and the money bags to impress them and gain their support. You need to be seen as credible. You must be able to discuss your ideas in a solution-oriented, vivid, and concise manner. You may follow Butman's plan, which is that *"you cannot expect to write a white paper and slap it on someone's desk. It is important to vary your messaging with something written,*

something spoken, something visual, and perhaps even something tangible."

You can also enlist the help and gain the support of those who do not need to fully understand what you are doing, like your parents, partners, friends, to be your support and your rock. They just need to provide you with the encouragement and the excitement you need to complete the task you have set out to do.

CHAPTER 10 : UNDERSTAND THAT THERE ARE AN EBB AND FLOW

Just because you are very inspired and motivated at the start of a project does not mean you will remain so excited until the completion of said project. There are going to be days you will tire, there will be days you just want to give up. There will be days you are willing to compromise on the quality of your project or the amount of work you are supposed to put in.

When you are not feeling motivated about your project, or you notice the excitement you started with is no longer there, do not panic. There is always a fluctuation in motivation when working on a project. It is entirely reasonable if you do not feel as excited in the middle of a project as you did in the beginning. Just stick it out, meditate,

doggedly continue, and the excitement will return.

Whenever motivation is lost, as it bound to happen, read about it. It will encourage you to keep trying. Read books, blog articles read various writeups about your goal and what you aim to achieve, read what inspired you in the first place. If you have been documenting your past successes, you can read about them or your written and set goals to encourage and motivate you.

Stick with your project. You do not want to be known as the person who gives up when the going gets tough. You made a commitment to your project, and this is what it means, to not give up, to stick through the ebbs, and the flow. You can also break down your task into small chunks to help you through the unmotivated phase you ae currently in.

CHAPTER 11: **DO NOT GIVE UP**

Once you have made a commitment to a project, you must see it through to the end. Many people gave up on their projects because *"they are no longer feeling it."* This is a very wrong mindset. No matter how difficult, uninspiring, boring it at seems, just stick it out.

Rather than give up, why not take a step back and clear your mind? You can do something beautiful for yourself to cheer yourself up and encourage yourself. While taking a breather, remember to time yourself so a 'little break' does not become the beginning of the end of your project. Also, remind yourself that this is neither the most challenging task, nor is it the first challenge thrown your way. Inspire yourself with the knowledge that you shall overcome this challenge as you have the previous ones.

Try to think of it as the bump in your story. You can't give up when you hit a bump, you just keep going forward. Remember that winners do not quit, and quitters do not win. It may be difficult now, but it is meant to be. If it were easy, everyone would do it. But not everyone can. You are one of the lucky few who had the guts to do it.

There are many people, who over the years before their big break, felt like giving up, but they didn't. They stuck with their goals and doggedly plowed, though. James Clear, a baseball player for over 17 years, also acknowledged that there were many times throughout his career that he was not motivated. To get his head back in the game, he developed a pre-game technique that got his head back in the game. *"I would grab a baseball and my glove. Jog out to the outfield foul pole.*

Jog across along the outfield wall. Stop at the opposite foul pole. Stretch hips and hamstrings. Jog back along the outfield wall. Toss lightly, working back to 75 feet or so.

Head to the bullpen. Stand one step behind the mound and toss three or four times from there to the catcher. Step up to the mound." He further went on to describe his pre-game routine. Why not develop your own pre-game routine that keeps you motivated whenever you feel like giving up? Stick with your plan and ride it out. The motivation will return.

CHAPTER 12: **BEGIN A LITTLE**

Starting with too much will backfire as you may soon feel overwhelmed, unmotivated, and unwilling to complete your task. Still, by starting small, you are building excitement. By starting low, you will not only expend less time and energy on your project, but you will also develop habits which will help you not only for your project but also to help you live a better life.

There is a great advantage to starting small, which is that you will no longer just be the person with ideas, you will the person taking steps to bring them to fruition. You will officially be moving towards your future in small-sized steps. To illustrate, when you meet someone new, you do not just ask them to marry you. You first go on dates. You start small, invitations for coffee, going to shows, or a walk. Short, meaningful acts that build a

relationship, that produces it to something more significant and long-lasting. Achieving your dreams works similarly. Just like humans, it is okay to attend to the little needs of your thoughts before you tackle the big problems. By starting small, you are dipping your toe into the pool, allowing yourself to get acclimated to the temperature of the water and the changes you may not have anticipated or observed when you viewed from the outside. You are now able to make changes to your proposed procedure and alter the plans to fit the current situation.

For instance, if you wish to exercise, it is best to start small rather than have an intense three-hour workout just because you are in the mood and regret it the next day. If you want to begin exercising on a long-term basis, it is best you start small with a two to ten-minute workout, and then gradually, as your body gets used to it, increase your workout hours. With this, you have a better chance of maintaining a workout schedule

rather than burning out too fast by biting too much.

CHAPTER 13: BUILD ON SMALL SUCCESSES

As stated earlier, there are numerous benefits to starting small. If you start low, you can quickly build on your successes. By setting seemingly ridiculous weekly goals, you are motivating yourself to continue working on your project. Little achievements like exercising for two minutes a day, writing 200 words in a week can make you flush with success and encourage you better than anything else to keep trying. You can then build on these successes by raising the bar a little higher to 500 words a week or five minutes of exercise routines a day. This will motivate and encourage you to keep trying. You can also write about your successes whenever you complete a task or set a goal.

A man named Ingvar Kamprad started his career as a salesman at a very tender age. He practiced sales by going door to door on

his bicycle, selling matches to the neighbors. As time moved on, he moved to sell Christmas decorations, fish, and ballpoint pens. When he was 17, he began his own company called IKEA. That company that started out as matches is now worth over 37 billion dollars. A lot of the big companies and successful businesses like Apple, Dell, Amazon, all follow the same pattern; they all started small. It makes the truth of the saying, *"Every master was once a beginner."* Bill Gates once said, *"Most people overestimate what they can do in one year and underestimate what they can do in ten years."* When you build on small successes, you will find yourself succeeding even beyond your expectations and discover abilities you did not know you had.

CHAPTER 14: CALL FOR HELP

A lot of people have an *"I can do all bad by myself"* mentality. They like to think they have it all figured out, and they do not need help. That is as far from the truth as it gets for all of us. We all need help sometimes.

Life is not always rosy, so whenever you are stuck and unable to get motivated or excited anymore, seek help. Sometimes, you are not strong enough to help yourself, and you need a shoulder to lean on. There are various forums available both online and offline that can help you rediscover yourself. Talking to people -be it family, friends, your local bartender, your next cab driver- can help you regain your mojo. Sometimes, you do not even have to listen to whatever advice they have to offer, sometimes the simple act of talking and letting things off your chest is what you need to become motivated. You can

also join a group or get a therapist.
There are also times when it is not the

words that are spoken but who the person who says them is all the motivation you need to get out of the slump you are in. So, do not be afraid to seek help whenever you need it.

What seems even scarier is if you are tired and you do not even know it. It is not easy to get back to the other side of the line when you are burnt out. It is not at all times that the mental exhaustion seems evident physically. You may be mentally worn down but still, carry on like everything is fine. You get out of bed and go to work with a smile on your face. Those who are not that close to you may not even know what is happening to you.

When you notice your passion begins to fade. You feel emotionally numb, when you are often disproportionally angry, and you are often exhausted just by spending a couple of minutes around people, it is best you call for help as you may be more than tired. You may be burning out.

CHAPTER 15: THINK ABOUT THE BENEFITS AND NOT THE DIFFICULTIES

Nothing good comes easy. One common mistake many people make is that they focus too much on the difficulties of the project they are about to embark on. There is no project, no task worthwhile that is not fraught with challenges and hurdles and bumps on the road. It is overcoming those challenges that make victory sweeter. It is only by slaying those dragons that you become a victor. If there are no challenges, then the task is not worth it. There is no way you can focus so much on the negatives or difficulties of a job and be excited to do it. The human mind as a way of exaggerating a problem until it seems too big and impossible.

Rather than think of the negatives, think of the benefits and how it will be of great advantage to you in the long run. Think

about the honor, think about the rush of pleasure you are going to derive when you prove your haters wrong. When you can visualize the success of your venture, you will see the benefits. Let that encourage you to keep pushing and working hard.

Thinking about difficulties is a form of negative thoughts. You tend to exaggerate the problems in your head or create absolutes and limitations on what you can and cannot do. Think instead about what you have to gain when you complete the project. Think about the accolades and
The benefits and let that drive you to succeed.

For example, just thinking about exercising is enough to make anyone shake their head and wince in imaginary pain, but thinking about the benefits, a fit, toned body, will encourage you to give it a try. Remember that there is no impossible, it is just a challenge waiting for you to overcome it. Think of the rewards of sweet victory and let that be your reason and your motivation.

CHAPTER 16: REPLACE NEGATIVE THOUGHT WITH POSITIVE ONES

Negative thinking narrows your focus and prevents your brain from seeing the other choices that surround you. You are going to end up feeling only negative emotions that will close your mind off from the outside world and suck all the joy and inspiration out of you. Positive thinking, on the other hand, allows for an increased ability to build and enhance your skills as well as develop resources that will be of excellent use to you always.

There is no way you are not going to have negative thoughts when dealing with a new project. You must monitor your thoughts as you think will eventually manifest. Recognize any negative thoughts and words and squash them immediately. Always follow your self-talk and begin positive

reinforcement whenever you catch yourself thinking negatively. Change all of your *"I can't do this; this is not going to work"* to *"I will do this. This is going to work. It is going to turn out great."* There is no snap way or flick switch that will change negative mindsets or kill the fears. Take it slowly and ease into change. You are not permanently stuck in one default setting. Remember that there is a difference between negative thoughts and reality and understand the difference. Do not bury your head in the sand and live a fairy tale life. No one said it is going to be easy, but it is definitely going to be possible. Do not let any negative vibe linger around you because it has a sneaky way of bursting your bubble.

CHAPTER 17: AIM HIGHER

One of the reasons for lack of motivation is that you are not aiming high enough. Does that make sense to you? Maybe not, but it is true. Just how motivated will a tenth grader be when presented with the academic challenges of a seventh-grader? Similarly, a person who often wrote 5,000 words a week for fun will not be motivated if he limits himself to writing 500 words a week for his novel. Pushing yourself, building new limits, setting new standards will provide you with the drive you need to complete your project. You want to get motivated? You want to finish your task in record time? Then you need to aim higher.

Push yourself, motivate yourself by aiming higher, and setting new limits. Do not listen to foolish thinking and limited lines of thought that tells you it is better to under-

promise and over-deliver than to set impossible tasks. That mindset will not allow for progress.

Aiming higher and higher will give you something to look forward to, a reason to get up each and every day, a task to accomplish, a reason to live. There is a feeling of happiness you derive when you complete a difficult task. It is the joy and the immense satisfaction that comes with mastering challenges. When you aim high, you generate for yourself, tremendous and elevated levels of excitement and anticipation that is unlike any other. Aiming higher will help you grow past your limitations. With big dreams, you get to learn new skills, acquire new knowledge, and make new records.

One of the most important and often, most neglected ingredients to success is the feeling of ecstasy that comes from succeeding at a challenging task. Setting big goals and expecting yourself to produce a fantastic result

will actually push you, give you a better chance of success. Even though it seems to run in the opposite direction of what other self-help gurus say, to grow and make something of yourself, you need the scary, the discomfort to push you to make the change you always wanted.

If you keep aiming higher, you will focus more on the long-term benefits, thus creating for yourself a better tomorrow. In the process of achieving your grand dreams, you will grow and learn more about yourself and the life that we are currently living. Creating a reality for yourself from your thoughts will help you overcome your limitations and create new records, both personal and otherwise.

CHAPTER 18: **KILL PROCRASTINATION**

The phrase *"procrastination is a thief of time"* is evergreen because it is true. One of the things that kill motivation very quickly is procrastinating. Ambiguity fuels procrastination. It is straightforward to procrastinate. It often starts by negotiating with yourself. *"I will start when I'm done with this episode"* or *"I'm having such a good time, I will start working on it when I get home"* or *"It is such a beautiful morning, let me just stay in bed for half an hour more."*

To achieve your goals and maintain your excitement, it is advisable that you set precise times to work on your project and make sure to stick to it. It can be challenging to get any work done if you are not organized enough. List and understand what you are going to work on for the slated hour. Do not decide to 'just wing it.' Invest in a planner or

calendar apps to help you keep track of the work you are supposed to do. For example, setting a particular time, thirty minutes after waking up in the morning and thirty minutes before bed, for exercise will ensure that you always go through your routines for the day. This set timetable will encourage you and motivate you to complete set tasks for the day, rather than leaving it up to whimsy and sitting around waiting to get driven to continue the job.

Also, breaking down your tasks to simple and easily achievable tasks will encourage you to complete your assignments on time. If you also set these easy goals with a specific timetable, it will help a great deal with procrastination.

While you are energized and fulling of spirit, it is best, you do the most difficult tasks first. That way, once you have gotten rid of the hardest part of the job, it will be easy to encourage yourself to finish up the rest of the work. Getting rid of distractions will help a

great deal in killing procrastination. It is straightforward to become distracted, especially when it is a task you do not want to do. Various forms of distractions will appear like the neighbor's barking dog or the song from the passerby's stereo. The smell of cookies from the kitchen or perhaps the biggest entertainment to millennials, the mermaid's call that is social media. When your phone is at hand and notifications start popping in, it becomes increasingly difficult to focus on anything else. Getting rid of distractions is the most important thing when you are trying hard to get a job done.

In the event, there is no one available to hold you accountable, you can create an incentive system for yourself to help you focus on your task. Once you have completed your task or reached a certain quota, you may take a break to recharge. You could also up the ante on the incentives to help you power through. For instance, you may award yourself that shoe you have been eyeing if you

complete your set tasks in the amount of time- slotted. If you perform above expectations and finish earlier, you may throw in the bracelet as well. The incentives will effectively kill

CHAPTER 19: SETTING SPECIFIC GOALS

Everybody has goals, everybody has plans, but the big question is, are those goals measurable? Are they attainable? Are they relevant? Are they time-bound? And most importantly, are they specific? Why are you killing yourself, determined to complete that task? Without answers to these questions, what you term as goals may just be empty dreams.

Setting specific goals helps you develop a sense of accomplishment and increase your self-worth. Setting goals will give you a long-term vision and also motivation in the short term. Having goals will help you organize your time and manage your resources to help you make the most out of your life. However difficult it might be to get started, once you are past that hurdle, you can build the biggest of dreams.

If you do not have a specific goal, you will find it challenging to complete your tasks. Specific goals answer the questions, *'who,' 'what,' 'when,' 'where'* and *'why.'* If your thoughts are not streamlined and your objectives clear, if you cannot answer these basic questions succinctly, then you will find it challenging to remain motivated for the completion of your project. Having vague plans like *"wake up earlier"* or *"exercise more"* or *"go out more"* will die a quick death if you are not specific in your structuring. Rather than make vague plans like that, why not make it more specific like *"wake up by 5:30"* or *"10 more pushups"* or *"visit these new establishments."*

Having a new specific plan will motivate you to want to try new things, push your limits, and make new personal records. Setting sharp, clearly defined goals will help you develop a sense of worth and boost your self-esteem. With specific goals, you can achieve attainable and notable success.

To set personal goals, you need to ask yourself the big picture question, "where do I see myself in five years?" when you have the big picture, you can then break them down into smaller, sizeable chunks. Break those chunks into considerable bits that are attainable and specific. Once you have your goals, you can begin developing your plans to achieve your lifetime goals.

Setting lifetime goals may be difficult for some people, as it is a broad scope. Create for yourself a catalog that covers the most important parts; career, finances, education, family, attitude, physical, pleasure, public service, in order of importance. Take your time in making these decisions and make sure the goals you set are the things you genuinely want to do and that they are not influenced by outside factors like your parents, family, employers or partners.

CHAPTER 20: MAKE HABITS YOUR MOTIVATIONS

Some so many people seem to have their lives together, right? They seem to have everything figured out, and they do not seem to break a sweat when they achieve the goals they set out to do. Well, it may be because those people have made a habit of their tasks. In whatever job you are trying to find the motivation to do, why not make a habit out of it? For instance, you want to wake up earlier, get used to set your alarms at the desired time. To become more fit, make a habit of exercising. To complete that writing task, get used to writing every day. Making your habit, your motivation will go a long way in making sure that you complete your job timely and efficiently. It will also provide a way to continue moving forward and making

headway with your project.

It is not an easy, magical task to develop a new habit. Dr. Maxwell Maltz, who was a plastic surgeon in the 1950s, noticed that it takes a minimum of 21 days to build a new practice. Upon this foundation, a lot of studies were carried out, and a lot of books written. In fact, this is the basis of the 21 days myth, which propagates that it takes only 21 days to develop a new habit.

Health psychology researcher at the University of London, Phillippa Lally, however, observed with her team that it takes anywhere from 18 days to 254 days to develop a new habit. Developing a new practice requires time and patience. It is dependent on several factors such as environment, personality, nature, and difficulty of the said task, and so on.

Undoubtedly, the best way to remain motivated is to continually work on something until it becomes a habit, no matter how long it

takes. To develop habits that lead to long life commitments, there are some baby steps you can talk to make the process easier and the journey smooth. One such acts are to commit for thirty days. It is not written in stone that at the end of the 30-day commitment, it will become part of you. Still, if you can commit to an activity every day for thirty days, then you can definitely make a habit out of it. At the end of the 30 days, you will have made it past the initial conditioning phase. Once you are past this phase, it becomes a whole lot easier to make a habit out of your tasks.

To make it to day 30, you have to do it every day. Consistency is key to developing a new habit. Without repetition, it does not become part of who you are, nor does it become a habit of yours. To create consistency, you have to start simple. Like it was discussed earlier, start small and build your successes. The same can be said for developing habits. You have to start small if you want to make it in the long run.

You may also get a buddy who is trying to develop a new habit, preferably the same as yours, so you can motivate each other and encourage each other. Having something that triggers you to performing your practice can also help you. It can be something as mundane as snapping your fingers each time you feel the urge to pick up a cigarette if you are trying to quit smoking.

Motivation is the key to life and success. Once you get motivated and inspired, you can do just about anything from something as simple as waking up ten minutes earlier to becoming the next Bill Gates.

Printed in Great Britain
by Amazon